WITHDRAWN

ETIQUETTE RULES!™

ETIQUETTE
AS A GUEST
AND AT PARTIES

JUSTINE CIOVACCO

rosen publishing's
rosen central®

NEW YORK

Published in 2017 by The Rosen Publishing Group, Inc.
29 East 21st Street, New York, NY 10010

Copyright © 2017 by The Rosen Publishing Group, Inc.

First Edition

Library of Congress Cataloging-in-Publication Data

Names: Ciovacco, Justine.
Title: Etiquette as a guest and at parties / Justine Ciovacco.
Description: New York : Rosen Publishing, 2017. | Series: Etiquette rules! | Includes bibliographical references and index.
Identifiers: ISBN 9781499464863 (library bound) ISBN 9781499464849 1 (paperback) | ISBN 9781499464856 (6-pack) Subjects: LCSH: Etiquette for children and teenagers—Juvenile literature. | Courtesy—Juvenile literature. | Children's parties—Juvenile literature.
Classification: LCC BJ1857.C5 C56 2017 | DDC 395.3—dc23

Manufactured in China

CONTENTS

I t was two weeks before Eddie's birthday party, and he was inviting people at school. His parents would be home during the party, but they agreed to let his friends take over their huge backyard until 10 p.m. Anna had never been invited to one of Eddie's famous parties, but she was thrilled when he invited her. "Everybody will be there," he said. "The place will be packed, but the party starts at 6:00. You should come!"

Anna went, also inviting her friend Joe along. They got there late, close to 9 p.m. Joe felt weird going since he didn't know Eddie, so he brought a copy of his favorite graphic novel wrapped in tissue paper. "He asked me to come, and he didn't tell me to bring anything," Anna told Joe.

In the backyard, Eddie greeted Anna. "Oh, it's late. I didn't think you were coming!" he said. He turned to Joe, thanked him for the gift, and then looked back at Anna. He was waiting for an introduction, but then said to Joe, "Hey, do I know you?"

"This is Joe," Anna said with shrug. "Hey, it's dark out here. Can I grab some candles inside?"

Eddie said he didn't know where any matches were or if his parents would want him to light candles. Anna went inside and found matches in the kitchen but no candles, until she looked in a living room cabinet. There, she took out a fancy candleholder with nine lights and an interesting-looking star decoration. The house was huge, so she really wanted to look upstairs. When she opened the first door, she saw two people in bed.

"Hello, are you Eddie's friend? Are you lost?" the slightly annoyed man asked. "And why are you carrying our menorah?"

It can be hard to fit in with a group anywhere, but parties can be especially awkward for some people since everyone is supposed to be happy and relaxed.

Anna realized that she had walked in on Eddie's parents' bedroom. After they explained the religious significance of the candleholder, Anna said, "Oops," before running outside.

By this time, Joe had introduced himself to people. He was handing out paper plates near the food table when Anna ran by. She was feeling silly and wanted to get the quiet party rolling. She started dancing and accidentally knocked over some soda and juice cartons. Anna laughed, but Eddie didn't. Joe looked around awkwardly. As for Eddie, he later thought to himself that maybe Joe would be invited to his next party, but Anna surely wouldn't.

Anna thought she was just having fun, so how could she have known that anything she did was wrong? The answer is etiquette. Anna really should have known better. Etiquette refers to the rules guiding the proper and polite way to behave. To some people these kind of rules are mostly common sense, but everyone needs a little help on matters of etiquette, including the etiquette of being a guest. How many of Anna's actions struck you as inappropriate? Let us take a closer look at what kind of etiquette you should adhere to as a guest at someone's home or at a party.

CHAPTER ONE

ETIQUETTE, MANNERS, AND POLITENESS

Human beings are not born knowing the complicated rules that make up good manners. Very young children don't know what the word "etiquette" means. But they get clues about how to behave from parents and other adults and older children, and they hopefully learn slowly but surely.

As we get older, people expect us to behave a certain way—the "right" way. We are expected to have manners and learn proper etiquette. We must know right from wrong so we don't annoy or offend people. But how do we know what is proper, and why would we care what people think?

MIND YOUR MANNERS

Merriam-Webster's Dictionary defines "manners" as "a characteristic or customary mode of acting." Of course, everyone has a different personality and behaves in different ways. The concept of manners means that people should behave in a way that is acceptable to most people. If we follow the rules of etiquette, people can see that we have manners—or at least that we are nice people. We aren't born knowing these rules, but it's best to learn them to help us feel comfortable and make others comfortable in social situations.

WHAT (NOT) TO DO WHEN MEETING THE QUEEN

If it seems nerve-wracking to meet your friends' parents for the first time or someone new at a party, imagine how awkward it is to meet royalty. Poor etiquette in those situations can sometimes turn into international news. Consider one incident involving the United States' First Lady, Michelle Obama.

In 2009, U.S. President Barack Obama and his wife, Michelle, visited Queen Elizabeth II at Buckingham Palace in England. There is a long list of rules, called protocols, people are expected to follow

When meeting a royal, like Queen Elizabeth II (here in green), it's correct for men to bow slightly—as UK prime minister David Cameron does above—and for women to curtsy.

when meeting British royals. One protocol is refraining from touching them. That seems easy enough, but what if they touch you? When the queen put her hand on Michelle Obama's back for a moment as they spoke, the First Lady warmly made the same return gesture. Media around the world—and those chiming in online—discussed whether or not she should have done that. Of course, heads of state have a little more leeway than us. They are not as tightly bound to these protocols.

President Obama and the First Lady did demonstrate good etiquette in other ways. The president bowed slightly when he met the queen, although only British citizens are technically required to do this. The couple brought a gift (a video iPod as well as a rare Broadway musical songbook). The First Lady covered her favored style of a sleeveless dress with a conservative sweater. Also, the couple posed for photographs with the queen with their arms in front of or behind them. In this case, they were mindful in avoiding touching her again!

A few more no-no's when meeting royalty:

- Don't touch. Let them offer a hand for a handshake first.
- Don't speak unless spoken to.
- Stop eating if they do.
- Don't turn your back to them.
- Don't dress sloppily. Dress formally and conservatively.
- Don't slurp your soup.

"Etiquette" is defined by *Merriam-Webster's* as "the conduct or procedure required by good breeding or prescribed by authority to be observed in social or official life." Proper etiquette shows people you are a good person who was raised right by your parents or other adults who may provide you with guidance.

Social situations—from simply visiting a friend's house to attending a party with a group you may not know—can be awkward. Even for people who usually feel comfortable and confident, knowing the proper etiquette makes a good

Many formal events involve adhering to etiquette. For example, there's a correct way to place silverware beside a plate.

impression. Behavior, appearance, and actions—before, during, and after an event—are important because they reflect on a person. These things are also important to friends, family, acquaintances, and even strangers who spend time with you.

GUESTS OF HONOR

When you visit a friend's house or attend a party there, you are a guest. Being a guest is an honor. It means people actually want you to spend time with them and that those people want

Greeting your host is one of the easiest parts of being a guest. After all, you know you are in a place you are wanted.

you to come into their homes and possibly meet their family members and friends. The respect and honor imparted to you as guest are both things you should likewise express right back.

GEORGE WASHINGTON'S RULES OF CIVILITY

Even great leaders need guidance. As a teen in the 1740s, the first president of the United States, George Washington, copied *The Rules of Civility and Decent Behaviour in Company and Conversation* **into his notebook. The 110 rules covered many of the proper social rules of his era. Although historians believe he may have copied them to practice penmanship, it is also clear Washington took many of them to heart.**

The rules were originally compiled by French Jesuits (a religious order within the Catholic Church) in the 1590s and then translated around fifty years later into English by Francis Hawkins, an English Jesuit. Washington did not have much formal education, so he sought to better himself by following the guidance of *The Rules.*

Topics covered in *The Rules* **included the principles of being civil to people in lower positions in society and respectful toward superiors. Many of the rules informed the reader how to act in public, such as Rule 12: "Shake not the head, Feet, or Legs roll not the Eyes lift not one eyebrow higher than the other wry not the mouth, and bedew no mans face with your Spittle, by approaching too near him when you**

Speak." Other rules covered professional and personal actions. For example, Rule 68 encouraged humility: "Go not thither, where you know not, whether you Shall be Welcome or not. Give not Advice without being Asked and when desired to do it briefly."

While leading the Continental army, Washington expected manners and cleanliness from his troops. He also promoted the rules to his family. He is said to have advised his stepgrandson, George Washington Parke Curtis, that, "while a courteous behavior is due to all, select the most deserving only for your friendships." This directly corresponds to Rule 56: "Associate yourself with Men of good Quality if you Esteem your own Reputation." The continued publication of his copy of *The Rules* has contributed greatly to his reputation as a gentlemanly leader.

It's important to be yourself so that you can feel comfortable. Making a good impression as a guest can help us:

- Gain confidence and acceptance as a person others can trust and enjoy spending time with
- Meet new people who can be friends or helpful associates at school, work, or just for fun
- Make our family and friends feel comfortable and even proud to be associated with us

For better or worse, people judge each other on first impressions. That is why it matters what you wear, if you

At a gathering, everyone can take turns being the focus of attention. Sometimes, it is nice just to hang out and listen to other people, rather than trying to dominate a circle of friends.

smile, what you say, how you say it, and how you behave. People often remember negative first impressions, too.

Making etiquette work for you means figuring out how you can be yourself while considering the feelings of others. Your actions will also affect the people who have invited you to their home or social gathering. Just like you want to feel comfortable and enjoy yourself, it is natural to want to make others feel the same way.

MYTHS AND FACTS

MYTH: Showing up early to help the host is always welcome.

FACT: Many hosts don't get dressed until they have the house or party site ready, and they may be embarrassed or frustrated at the thought of having to entertain you early. Find out ahead of time if showing up early will be helpful, or at least not a problem.

MYTH: The host has everything planned and doesn't need help.

FACT: Everyone likes to be helped, especially hosts because they are outnumbered by guests at parties! Feel free to ask about specific ways you can help ("Can I grab a vase for you? Want me to put more chips in the bowl?"), so you don't get stuck doing things you may not want to do.

MYTH: Handwritten thank-you notes are old-fashioned.

FACT: Some younger people may feel that way, but—even in their eyes—a handwritten note will stand out and be remembered.

CHAPTER TWO

WHAT TO KNOW BEFORE YOU GO

T
here are many things you can do before you attend a party or visit someone's house that will make the experience better for you and your host. A little planning ahead can help you avoid awkwardness or uncomfortable feelings.

TO RSVP OR NOT RSVP?

Have you ever gotten an invitation that asks you to RSVP? Those four letters are shorthand for the French phrase *Répondez, s'il vous plaît,* meaning "Please reply." They are often followed by a date you should respond by. You should always respond by that date. Even if you are not sure you can attend, at least let the host know what is holding up your reply. Your response is important so the host can be sure there is enough space for you and enough food and drinks for all guests.

With a formal invitation, such as a wedding, a reply card is often included, often with a self-addressed and stamped return envelope. Send it back and, when asked, note if you are bringing a guest (if the invitation is sent to you "and guest," you may add one) and your meal choice (for example, a meat or vegetarian option). If the invitation comes by email, you can reply by email. If a phone number is provided and you are asked to call, you should try to call during a reasonable hour and not too early or too late in the day.

Sometimes an invitation notes "regrets only." This means you need to respond only if you cannot attend. A short, polite email, note, or phone call will always be appreciated so the host doesn't feel the need to spend money and time preparing for guests who have no intention of coming.

The Emily Post Institute, an organization dedicated to teaching proper etiquette, suggests there are only a few reasons to change an RSVP once you've given an answer. Their experts note that changing a "yes" to a "no" is only acceptable due to illness or injury, a death in the family, or an unavoidable professional or business conflict. If necessary, call your hosts immediately. Changing a "no" to a "yes" is acceptable only if it will not upset the hosts' plans.

Invitations should give guests everything they need to know about attending the party. Once a guest gets an invitation, the next step is in his or her hands.

WHAT TO ASK AHEAD OF TIME

Although hosts should provide you with enough information about when and where to come, you may have important questions that can be answered ahead of time. You can ask about almost anything, if you do so politely.

Can you can bring a guest? Think it over carefully because you may make your host feel awkward if he or she simply doesn't have enough space or money to add another guest to the event. If you want to bring a friend, you should ask

A small gift or food to eat at the gathering are welcomed by most hosts. These things show thoughtfulness and appreciation.

the host directly. Doing so by email or text will give the host enough time to consider your request and respond.

Bringing a guest to a party, especially a formal event, is trickier. After all, another guest is another person to fit into a set space and perhaps feed, as well. Sometimes invitations will state your name "and guest," which means a guest is clearly invited. In these cases, it's polite to let your host know who the guest will be.

If an additional guest is not mentioned, you can try to politely find out if it is OK to bring guests. You may start by asking a friend if he or she knows if you can bring guests. A friend that has already obtained that information can save you a lot of time worrying about how to ask.

You can also talk to the host to get a feel for the party. In a phone call or (for less formal events) an email, you may express your thanks for the invitation and make small talk, asking how big the event will be and if you should bring anything. This may lead to the host mentioning that you can bring a guest, or it may be a smooth way to mention that you know your friend Joe would love to come, if the host feels comfortable with more people.

GUEST DRESS CODE

Another important question is what you should wear. Obviously, your friends see you often, but you may want to dress up a bit if you will, for example, be joining their parents for dinner. Dressing up could mean jeans with no holes or even that jeans are not acceptable. Asking your friends what they will wear is an easy way to decide. If you are unsure what to wear to formal events, consult the internet. For example, if you are nonreligious and unsure what to wear to a celebration held by a friend who is Jewish or Muslim, an online search can give you the answers you need.

Derek Blasberg, editor at large of the fashion magazine *Harper's Bazaar* and author of the etiquette book *Very Classy*, advises guests to always dress their best. "When in doubt, dress up," he suggested in *Oprah* magazine. "But if you've missed the mark, smile more and make up for your lack of attire with witty conversation."

WHAT TO DO WHEN YOU'RE NOT INVITED

Not everyone gets invited to every gathering and party they'd like to be invited to. Although that may hurt, the way you handle it can make you feel better. Stay cool. You just may be invited to the next event—or you may realize you are better off not going even if you are invited next time.

First, think about why you were not invited. You don't want to spend too long on this, but ask yourself: Did I say or do anything wrong? Why might certain guests be invited? Could it be a mistake? Think about past conversations and actions. Then try to let it go. You cannot control how people feel.

Next, accept that you are not invited and avoid resentment. Acting upset about it in front of others only makes you look bad. Instead, plan something fun to do during the time you would have spent at the event. You deserve to enjoy yourself and to make plans with others who want your company.

SHOULD YOU BRING SOMETHING?

One of the more thoughtful questions you can ask ahead of time is: What can I bring? It shows you appreciate the invitation and are thinking of the other person's needs. Often, it is recommended that you bring something if it is an informal event—like a birthday party. Sometimes the host will specify what to bring, like drinks, snacks, desserts, or a dish. Other times, you may have more leeway.

A good way to decide is by finding out via conversation, email, or text. Many hosts nowadays use social media

Sometimes, hosts have planned every detail of a meal, so it is good to ask them what—if anything—you can bring to help. You want to avoid bringing what they already have.

platforms like Facebook, Twitter, or Instagram to invite guests. These virtual invites may include many details about the cuisine planned. You can make sure not to double up on things. You risk probably attracting more attention to your own dish or snack than what the host provides, which is a no-no.

Bring things that everyone enjoys. Remember that foods should be event-appropriate. Whether it is avoiding certain cuisine—for instance pork, which may be barred for religious reasons—or simply not bringing fast food to a formal dinner, put thought into your food choices as a guest.

One faux pas is bringing something that is the same as or similar to what will already be there. Also, it is important to note that some people have allergies to foods, so you should ask if any are known or just consider bringing foods without nuts or treats that are gluten-free—either of which will be welcomed by people with common allergies. These days, it is customary to inform your host about such ingredients. Hosts will likely make it known ahead of time, too. It is the height of politeness to respect their wishes.

BRINGING A GIFT

Besides party supplies and food, you may want to bring a gift for the host (especially if it is his or her birthday party) or something everyone can enjoy at the party. When visiting a friend for the first time, a little gift can be a thoughtful gesture. The host will be happy just to see people that have been invited, but it's a nice surprise token of appreciation or friendship.

Remember that it's important to consider the hosts' culture and lifestyle when visiting their home or attending their party. If you are bringing a unique gift, get a second opinion: you may ask friends or family if a gift you want to bring seems right for the occasion and the receiver. You wouldn't want to bring a platter of meat to a vegetarian's house. Neither would you bring a religious artifact or anything else that might be misconstrued.

TEN QUESTIONS TO ASK A PARTY PLANNER

1. What makes a great guest?
2. What makes a great host?
3. How do you know whom to invite?
4. Is there a polite way to ask if you can come to a party?
5. What is the rudest thing a guest could do?
6. What should a guest do if everyone brings a gift except him or her?
7. What should a guest do if he or she is under- or overdressed?
8. When you plan a party, do you plan for more guests than you've invited?
9. Is there a tactful way to leave, interrupt, or end a party conversation?
10. How do I behave at formal events versus informal ones?

CHAPTER THREE

BEING A GOOD GUEST

As a guest at a friend's house, you have some flexibility in making arrangements about when you'll visit. You have less flexibility when a group of people are also invited to attend the friend's house at the same time for a party or a gathering. And you have even less flexibility when attending a formal event, like a wedding or other ceremony.

If a friend invites you over any time, you should feel free to suggest a time if your friend clearly doesn't seem to mind when you come over. Likewise, the friend may suggest one, too. Or, feel free to ask her to set a concrete time. It is her house, after all. If you are meeting in the morning or at night, then you should ask what time everyone wakes up or goes to bed in the house so you come over at a time when you are welcome. Also calculate when everyone will be up and about and finished with their morning routine. Coming over right when people are likely to be getting ready for bed is also not recommended.

When it comes to parties, arrive fifteen minutes before or fifteen minutes after the time the party is supposed to start. If you get to the location earlier than that and know your host fairly well, you may call or text to see if you can come in to help him or her prepare for the other guests.

If you are more than an hour early, you may find the host hasn't gotten him- or herself ready yet because of the time it

A good guest is eager to help the host. Even if help is not needed, a host will appreciate that you asked because sometimes there can be a lot to do to keep all guests fed and comfortable.

takes to prepare the food, clean the house, and other tasks. In that case, unless you know the person well, you should figure out a way to spend the time so you don't make your host (or his or her parents) feel rushed or awkward because they feel they need to entertain you earlier than expected.

If you are more than 15 minutes late, that's not great, but don't sweat it. Call or text your host and briefly explain that you are late and when you expect to join the gathering. This way, no one worries about you or waits to do things if you'll be significantly late. By always thinking of your hosts and other guests, you are on your way to being a good guest.

GIFT IDEAS THAT WON'T BREAK THE BANK

You don't have to spend much to bring your host a gift, or to help out with party supplies. Here are some ideas:

For a small gathering at a friend's house, if it is a special occasion:

- **A book (new is best, but used is OK for close friends)**
- **Flowers (bonus points if you present them to the adults in charge!)**
- **Food or nonalcoholic drinks**

A simple gift of flowers can brighten anyone's day. They are not just for girls—guys are often happily surprised at a gift of flowers, too.

For a large gathering or party at a friend's house:

- Flowers (include a simple vase or bring a potted plant so the host doesn't have to fetch a vase)
- Food or nonalcoholic drinks (after you ask if they need anything to entertain)
- A gift card
- Something you have made by hand for the house or host (perhaps a ceramic vase or a small craft)
- Something you buy for the house or family (perhaps a picture frame or a box of chocolates)

For a gathering held by someone you don't know:

- Any of the above, but be careful to ask a friend the kinds of things the hosts likes first.

A FEW MUST-HAVE MANNERS

While at the party, the Emily Post Institute suggests that being a "willing participant" will make things go smoother for you and your host. This means you should feel free to take food or drinks when the host suggests. Not doing so will make the host feel the need to come over to you and see if you need something. Good hosts always check if everyone is enjoying themselves. Similarly, be open to whatever activities hosts or other guests suggest or plan out. Even if you feel ridiculous playing pin the tail on the donkey or another party game, be gracious and enthusiastic. It is impolite and unsettles people if you're the one person at a party not participating or having fun.

LENDING A HAND

Good guests also help out. The host—and perhaps his parents or family members helping host—have much to do while entertaining. You can generally express that you are willing to help. Yet the Emily Post Institute suggests you be specific when you offer to help, such as "I'd be happy to prep the salad or fill the water glasses." This way, the host doesn't even have to stop to think of what you can do—or feel awkward asking you to do something while wondering if you really won't want to do it. The fact that you asked will be appreciated, even if the host says no help is needed.

PRIVACY AND BOUNDARIES

Another absolute must is respecting the privacy and property of your hosts and other guests. At a house gathering or party, that is especially important because you are often able to roam freely into areas the hosts would never want a stranger to visit. Never enter a room with a closed door, unless it's a bathroom—and then you should knock first. Never look through the host's or other guests' belongings, even if something looks really interesting. Even if you innocently pick up something, it can be awkward to be seen with it in your hands. Some etiquette experts even believe it is a breach of conduct to look curiously into the rooms of someone's house even if the doors are open and you are just passing through.

Unless a host says you can look in a cabinet or in the refrigerat[or], [do] not open them. Things behind doors are not always meant to be seen by everyone, nor are people's possessions complimentary.

BEING MINDFUL

In general, pay attention to your host and the other invited guests. Be open to meeting new people and getting to know friends and acquaintances better. Turn off your phone, or at least put it on vibrate, if you think you can handle the vibration alert without constantly interrupting a conversation. Ideally, you should be able to leave it with your jacket or bag if these can be left somewhere secure.

If you do have to use your phone, the polite thing to do is apologize and briefly explain why you need to take a call or respond to a text. Then excuse yourself and move somewhere private to speak or text without disturbing or blocking the way of others.

GETTING IN ON THE ACTION

Introverts and extroverts act differently at gatherings. Introverts are naturally quiet and may want to hang out with familiar people or perhaps one or two new people at a time. Extroverts are usually happy to make new friends, talk to everyone, dance and sing, and maybe even make a speech or hold court in front of a large group.

So what if you sang too loud or made an awkward speech or even got a little too out of hand at the last gathering? Hey, it happens to everyone at some point. You can start by apologizing to people for your behavior last time. Although you want to show you care, a little humor about it may make things less awkward: "Hey, everyone, don't worry, I hurt my knee training for the Olympics, so no dancing on tables tonight!" or "I'm all talked out from the long speech I gave at the last party. Tonight, I'm the official listener."

GOOD BEHAVIOR

Of course, sometimes your own behavior is not the issue. Keep an eye on guests you bring. First, you want your guests to have a good time and feel included. It's important to make introductions to people your guest may not know (an example of a good icebreaker: "Hi Rosie, this is Roberto. He's a big movie fan, too."). This helps people feel comfortable getting to know new people.

The best part of a party is connecting with other people. A good guest doesn't just whisper with one person the whole night. He or she should let others in on the conversation.

Guests you invite reflect on you. You are ultimately responsible whether your guest behaves well. Feel free to tell your guest if something he or she is doing is wrong. After all, whether your guest is a friend, relative, or boyfriend/girlfriend, if he or she is not a good guest, you won't look like a good guest.

Another way to be a good guest is to avoid trouble. Don't bring drugs or alcohol with you and avoid anyone that brings them to a gathering or party. Even if parents allow children to serve alcohol, always remember that they are breaking the law. The consequences could be dire if something goes wrong, and you could end up taking heat you did not ask for.

Furthermore, avoid critiquing a host or a party while you are at the party. With everyone standing around, people are likely to overhear you. Keep in mind that hosting is difficult. Don't you find it tough to make all of your friends and family members happy? A host is usually eager to do exactly that within the few hours invited guests have come to be part of his or her gathering.

CHAPTER FOUR

THE PARTY AND AFTERWARD

Whether you are having a good time or not, the way you leave a gathering and what you do after it are important to the host. If you want to be invited back, you'll want to make a smooth exit and offer some kind post-party appreciation.

SAYING GOOD-BYE

It is polite to stay at a party for at least an hour or two, but you never want to overstay your welcome. Signs that the party is over include the music being turned off, the brightest lights being turned on, and the food and drinks being put away. In fact, if you see any of these happen, you should jump in to help clean up. Even if you are ready to leave, but waiting for a ride home, a little clean-up time will make tired hosts happy.

It is generally respectful to say good-bye to your host—or at least one of them if there are more than one. If you are leaving a gathering at a friend's house or a party paid for by a friend's parents, a quick expression of thanks goes a long way, and it is often especially appreciated by adults.

TOPICS TO TALK ABOUT

An important part of hanging out with people is talking to them. A good conversation keeps old and new friends entertained and helps people get to know more about each other. What follows are a few conversation ideas.

At a gathering of friends:

- Funny things that happened at school
- A funny Internet video
- A new song that you just heard
- A song you can't get out of your head
- Something funny your family member did (if it's not too embarrassing!)

At a gathering with people you don't know well:

- What school you each attend or what jobs you have
- An interesting meal you had recently (perfect for when you start to eat)
- Your favorite places to eat in the local area
- Where everyone grew up and where they live now
- Whether or not everyone has brothers and/or sisters—then you can talk about them or discuss what it's like to be an only child
- How you know the host
- The weather (a classic conversation starter!)

After a party, there is always something to clean up. Besides cleaning up your own mess, offer to help the host put away food and decorations.

For small gatherings of a dozen people of less, it is best to thank the host in person. If a party has more than a dozen guests and the host is busy, he or she may not be upset if you slip out. Still, you should send a text or email within a couple of hours to express appreciation. "What a great party! Thank you so much for having us" is fine, but it will stand out even more if you can mention a highlight—perhaps a favorite food you ate or a person you met.

WHY DO WE CARE WHAT EMILY POST SAYS?

Emily Post is one of the best-known names in etiquette advice. Born in 1872 to a wealthy family, she grew up as Emily Price in Baltimore, Maryland, and was homeschooled until her family moved to New York. There, she attended a finishing school. These schools—more popular back then but still in existence today—teach people how to properly behave in social situations, how to dress, how to greet people, how to set a table, and so on. In her day, these schools were only for women and were sometimes called charm schools.

Post enjoyed writing novels as well as magazine and newspaper articles on travel, architecture, and interior design. At age fifty in 1922, she published her first etiquette book, *Etiquette in Society, in Business, in Politics, and at Home*. It became a best seller and has been updated and reprinted many times.

The success of her first book made Post an expert on manners and social etiquette. Yet she didn't always follow what was expected in society: as a young girl she was told well-bred women could not work. Not only did she work, but she became a celebrity known for her work, providing timeless advice in books, in print media, and on her radio program.

In 1946, Post founded the Emily Post Institute, which today is led by her great- and great-great-grandchildren. Now thoroughly modern, the institute

Emily Post is seen here on the phone in her living room circa 1940. You can probably safely bet she did not put her feet up on the couch as a guest in someone else's house.

has a website and podcasts on which the Posts teach etiquette. As the institute explains on its website, "Whether it's a handshake or a fist bump, it's the underlying sincerity and good intentions of the action that matter most."

POSTING PICTURES

"I always ask myself: Is the person who organized the party on Twitter, Facebook, or tweeting from the dinner table themselves?" said Derek Blasberg, author of the best-selling etiquette book *Very Classy*, in *Oprah* magazine. "If the answer is yes, game on . . . But if someone is notoriously secretive, it's always better to err on the side of discretion." That said, make sure all images you post—even if you have permission to do so—are flattering and tame enough for anyone else to see. A safe bet is to think about who might be upset or embarrassed by a picture. Imagine the worst-case scenario of one of these people seeing each image: friends who weren't there, boyfriends or girlfriends, someone's parents, and teachers. When in doubt, ask the host if he or she thinks a picture is okay to post.

TAKE NOTE

A thank-you note or even a small gift (especially if you forgot to bring one and saw that everyone else did) is a nice follow-up to a party. As mentioned, a quick text or email the night of the gathering will make a host smile.

Formal gatherings and larger parties—including baby and wedding showers, weddings, bar mitzvahs, quinceañeras, and the like—can be followed up with a more polite and formal handwritten note card expressing thanks. As the Emily Post Institute explains, "For dinner parties, big favors, an actual gift, or being a houseguest, handwritten thank-you notes are your best bet for an expression of warm, heartfelt thanks."

If you have a great time at a party, let your host know. Of course, it is also nice if the host shows appreciation for guests coming for a visit.

APPRECIATE IT

Being a guest is an honor, and it shows the host trusts you and wants to spend time with you. When you are a good guest at a gathering or party for family members, friends, or worthy acquaintance, you make them proud or at least happy to invite you back.

An invitation to a party or gathering is a key to enjoy time with people you like, love, or want to get to know. You never know whom you may meet. Being a good guest just may lead to more invitations. So keep in mind the most important rules of attending parties and visiting with people: be helpful and kind, and enjoy yourself.

acquaintance A person one knows only slightly or not very well.

appreciation To be grateful for, or to see the worth, quality, or significance of something.

awkward Describes a situation or behavior causing embarrassment.

conversation The act of two or more people speaking with each other.

etiquette The rules governing the proper way to behave in a given situation.

expert Someone showing special skill or knowledge gained from training or experience.

faux pas An embarrassing or tactless act or remark in a social situation.

flexibility The ability to change or adapt to something, such as a situation.

formal Following or agreeing with established form, custom, or rule.

gathering A bringing together of people.

impression Something that affects someone strongly or deeply.

invitation The written, printed, or spoken expression by which a person is invited to an event.

manners Social conduct or rules of conduct as shown in the prevailing custom.

occasion Something that brings about an event, such as a birthday.

permission The approval of a person in authority.

politeness Showing consideration and courtesy.

regret To be keenly sorry for, such as sorry to be unable to come to a party.

RSVP Refers to an invitation that requests a yes or no on whether you plan to attend an event.

tactful Having tact, the ability to deal with others in sensitive or awkward situations.

FOR MORE INFORMATION

Canadian School of Protocol & Etiquette
380 Wellington Street
6th Floor, Suite 600
London, ON N6A 5B5
Canada
(519) 964-2752
Website: http://www.thecanadianschoolofprotocol.com
This organization helps individuals and groups learn communications
and etiquette skills. The experts on the team offer classes and
speeches to kids, teens, and adults on a variety of etiquette
subjects, and the site includes videos to help deal with everyday
etiquette-related situations.

Elaine Swann Enterprises, LLC
1976 S. La Cienega Boulevard, Suite 565
Los Angeles, CA 90034
(323) 539-8911
Website: http://www.elaineswann.com
Elaine Swann is a lifestyle and etiquette expert who has appeared
on numerous TV shows, including the Today Show, and written
a number of books and articles on the subject. Her site includes
her blog (http://www.elaineswann.com/etiquette-expert-blog).

The Emily Post Institute
444 South Union Street
Burlington, VT 05401
(802) 860-1814
Website: http://emilypost.com
The Emily Post Institute is run by the descendants of noted etiquette
expert Emily Post. The site offers information and suggestions
for all kinds of etiquette topics, including gifts and thank-you
notes.

International Association of Professional Etiquette Consultants
167 Midland Place S.E.
Calgary, Alberta T2X 1N1
Canada
Website: https://www.iapcollege.com/program/membership-
etiquette-consultants
The IAPEC professional organization has offices in Princeton, New
Jersey, as well as Alberta, Canada. It is run by the International
Association of Professions Career College (IAP Career College),
which aims to offer affordable online certificate programs for
dream careers.

The Mitchell Organization
620 N. 34th Street, # 508
Seattle, WA 98103
(215)284-7975
Website: http://themitchellorganization.com
The Mitchell Organization provides employers and employees
guidance on making presentations, managing business
relationships, understanding cultural etiquette, and more.
Among the website's resources are articles on etiquette topics.

WEBSITES

Because of the changing number of internet links, Rosen Publishing has
developed an online list of websites related to the subject of this book.
This site is updated regularly. Please use this link to access this list:

http://www.rosenlinks.com/ER/guest

FOR FURTHER READING

Barnes, Bob. *Good Manners for Today's Kids.* Eugene, OR: Harvest House Publishers, 2010.

Eberly, Sheryl. *365 Manners Kids Should Know.* New York, NY: Harmony Books, 2011.

Ephron, Delia. *Do I Have to Say Hello? Aunt Delia's Manners Quiz for Kids and Their Grownups.* New York, NY: Blue Rider Press, 2015.

Fulcher, Roz. *Mind Your Manners!: A Kids Guide to Proper Etiquette.* Mineola, NY: Dover Publications, 2013.

Furgang, Kathy. *Netiquette: A Student's Guide to Digital Etiquette.* New York, NY: Rosen Publishing, 2011.

Johnson, Dorothea, and Liv Tyler. *Modern Manners: Tools to Take You to the Top.* New York, NY: Potter Style, 2013.

Packer, Alex J., Ph.D. *How Rude!: A Teen Guide to Good Manners, Proper Behavior, and Not Grossing People Out.* Golden Valley, MN: Free Spirit Publishing, 2014.

Post, Peggy, et al. *Emily Post's Etiquette, 18th Edition.* New York, NY: William Morrow, 2011.

Post Senning, Cindy, and Peggy Post. *Prom and Party Etiquette.* New York, NY: Collins Publishing, 2010.

Reynolds, Kate E. *Party Planning for Children and Teens on the Autism Spectrum.* London, England: Jessica Kingsley Publishers, 2012.

Richa, Joelle. *Guide to Good Manners: From Precious Parents to Precious Kids.* Hobert, NY: Hatherleigh Press, 2015.

Rossi, Patricia. *Everyday Etiquette.* New York, NY: St. Martin's Griffin, 2011.

The Emily Post Institute. "About Emily Post". Retrieved April 5, 2016. http://emilypost.com/about/emily-post.

The Emily Post Institute. "Advice: Different Ways to Say Thank-You." Retrieved April 5, 2016. http://emilypost.com/advice/different-ways-to-say-thank-you.

The Emily Post Institute. "Advice: Party Etiquette Tips for Hosts and Guests." Retrieved April 5, 2016. http://emilypost.com/advice/party-etiquette-tips-for-hosts-and-guests.

The Emily Post Institute. "Advice: Should I Bring a Hostess a Gift?" Retrieved April 5, 2016. http://emilypost.com/advice/should-i-bring-a-hostess-gift.

Gaskill, Laura. "Modern Party Etiquette for Hosts and Guests." Houzz.com. Retrieved April 5, 2016. http://www.houzz.com/ideabooks/20070565/list/modern-party-etiquette-for-hosts-and-guests.

Glassman, Adam. "What This Party Pro Knows About Being a Fabulous Host (or Guest)." Oprah.com, November 22, 2011. http://www.oprah.com/entertainment/Holiday-Parties-Party-Etiquette.

Kahn, Huma. "Royal Etiquette: Do's and Don'ts When Meeting Her Majesty." ABC News, April 1, 2009. http://abcnews.go.com/Politics/International/story?id=7228105&page=1.

PBS Parents Online. "Birthday Party Etiquette." Retrieved April 5, 2016. http://www.pbs.org/parents/birthday-parties/tips_post/birthday-party-etiquette.

Ponikowski, Marissa Stapley. "Birthday Party Etiquette." Retrieved April 5, 2016. http://www.todaysparent.com/kids/birthday-parties/birthday-party-etiquette.

Post Senning, Cindy, and Peggy Post. *Prom and Party Etiquette.* New York, NY: Collins Publishing, 2010.

Real Simple. "Proper Etiquette for Every Occasion: Manners for Parties." Retrieved April 5, 2016. http://www.realsimple.com/work-life/work-life-etiquette/proper-etiquette/proper-etiquette-2.

Schoorl, Katrina. "The Rules of Civility and Decent Behaviour" (http://www.mountvernon.org/digital-encyclopedia/article/the-rules-of-civility-and-decent-behaviour).

ABOUT THE AUTHOR

Justine Ciovacco has written more than sixty nonfiction books and hundreds of articles for young people. Her writing has been published by Discovery Channel School Books, Scholastic Inc., Reader's Digest Books for Young Families, *National Geographic*, *Time for Kids*, Dorling Kindersley, SmartLab, *World Almanac for Kids Online*, and Disney, among others.

PHOTO CREDITS

Cover, pp. 7, 16, 24, 33 (top) Aaron Amat/Shutterstock .com; cover (bottom) Henglein and Steets/Cultura/Getty Images; p. 5 Lisa Peardon/The Image Bank/Getty Images; p. 8 Max Mumby/Indigo/Getty Images; p. 10 Tamara Staples/Stone/Getty Images; pp. 11, 39 Jupiterimages/Photolibrary/Getty Images; p. 14 Ron Levine/Stone/Getty Images; p. 17 Mosquito/DigitalVision Vectors/Getty Images; p. 18 Iakov Filimonov/Shutterstock.com; p. 21 Paper Boat Creative/DigitalVision/Getty Images; p. 25 Portra Images/Taxi/Getty Images; p. 26 Peter Muller/Cultura/Getty Images; p. 29 MoMo Productions/Stone/Getty Images; p. 31 Chris Ryan/OJO Images/Getty Images; p. 35 Kevin Fitzgerald/The Image Bank/Getty Images; p. 37 FPG/Archive Photos/Getty Images.

Designer: Nicole Russo; Editor: Philip Wolny; Photo Researcher: Philip Wolny